THE TALE OF A PAPER FLOWER

A TALE TOLD THROUGH 25 POEMS

ARPAN NAITHANI

ISBN 979-888555622-4

Contents

Contents

Preface

A paper flower is born fragile. Fragmented even.

Compared to a flower tucked between the yellowed pages of an old journal, a paper flower doesn't signify beauty immediately. It requires your fingertips to handle each petal, carefully assessing the fragments of a memory, inflicted with equal amounts of despair, longingness and relief.

I wrote Paper Flowers in 2018, a few years after having avoided mourning a personal loss. New experiences came forth, new people introduced themselves, and yet the heart would go back to those memories perfectly preserved in my mind.

Not out of a sense of pain, but with an intent to remember where I had come from, and the person I am now.

This collection, being a bittersweet reminiscence of a time when I truly felt alive, is a personal ode in the form of a paper flower - an existence which has reached its peak of beauty and yet, refuses to decay over time.

1. Paper Flowers

Once again,
I look at these trees
That don't seem to shed
Their leaves.
I'm reminded
Of the paper flowers
I left at our grave,
Wrinkled by the wind
But still intact.

2. Nothing Coming Apart at the Seams

The metropolis
Was teeming
With
Isles of longing,
Isolated,
And lost to the others,
In the mazy currents
Of the sea of thought.
The howls and screams
Silently reside
On the cusp of the lips
Of good old pleasantries.
For now,
Nothing
Coming apart at the seams.
The 3 AM wind
Rustles
The infant leaves,
And my heart flutters
For once,

To remind me
Of the flock of seagulls
That never returned
In the wake
Of the perennial winter
Within.
Or was it
The other way round?
The raindrops start falling
As some kind
Of sarcastic applause
For yet another
Train of thought.
For now,
Nothing
Coming apart at the seams.

3. When Autumn Arrived

I knew
Autumn had arrived
As an ache,
Lashing within
The walls of your lips.
You were staring
At some abstract art
That others had lavished
With pedantic praise.
Just observe
The brutality of the brushwork.
Oh, but in such good taste.
The tears
You knew would never come
Out and play,
Coagulated
Within your skin.
Just like
When you were nine,
Smashing up
Your sandcastle
Before

The sea could set it to siege.
The seeds you swallowed
In April,
In silence,
Had slept through the summer,
And sprouted into sadness.
I saw you
Leave the name
Of your lost lover
To rust,
On the back
Of a fallen leaf,
And watch time
Eat
Into an earnest promise
Of eternity.
(Entry #7,
Healthy defense mechanisms.
Death by poetry)

4. The Umbrella Seller

She sat by her stall,
Dutifully,
For it was time.
When the sadness touched
The stratosphere,
And made the clouds precipitate,
It rained.
She sold the umpteenth umbrella
Unconditionally,
To the melancholy man,
For it was time.
It was some kind of blue,
A bit jaded,
Faded,
And then rain will leave it
With patches of a weary white.
The way everyone feels
Perhaps
Internally,
About the eternal notion
Of demand and supply.
Her heedless heart,

Didn't mind getting wet.
The water made the wounds
Disappear,
Externally.
But on the nights
It didn't rain,
The stall was wrapped in silence.
And she bled words which wilted by the morning,
Into what they called poetry.
One day,
It rained indefinitely,
But no one came,
And her heart bled
Into bouquets
Of unwritten verses,
Till there was nothing left,
And she finally slept
Soundly.
The coroner said
She died of natural causes.

5. The Necklace

From the corner of my eye,
I noticed
That you've stopped wearing
The necklace
Made out of the beads,
Made from the bokeh of shooting stars.
Have you lost it to Forever?
That fickle friend,
Wagered in a game,
Playing for time,
Against fate?
Or do you still keep it safe
Somewhere,
Beyond the palindrome of a promise,
Unmade?

6. Half Mast

You lay
In a bastion
Guarded by gilded
Guns,
And I,
Invisible to the eye,
Waste away,
With what remained
Of my white flag,
Flying at half mast.

7. Rose Unsent

Am I an untaken chance
Or just an unwelcome
Glance?
Then again,
I never quite figured
Out.
What happens to a rose
Unsent,
Withheld
At the penultimate
Second,
On the account
Of what it all could
Be?

8. Sisyphus

Again we meet,
Like the hands of the clock that complete
Revolutions within minutes and hours.
Futility never moved so fast,
Through a blizzard of trading lights.
A timeless memorial to that time,
When the digital films were daguerreotypes.
Far into the enemy lines,
The ghosts of yesterday have arrived
Fashionably late.
The dregs of our humanity lie
And so do I,
By chasing cars and changing channels.
It's a set piece rigged for self-destruction.
Who am I,
But a troubled troubadour playing truant,
Who has learnt to love the bomb?
When I think of your face
Or perhaps when you think of mine,
Trapped within that fading photograph,
Ravaged by the grime,
Partly unwashed by the tears unshed,

Belying what really transpired.
I hope those silhouettes manage a smile.
After all, one must imagine Sisyphus happy.

9. Deconstruction

Would you unwrite the story,
Half-heartedly, half-written
When you wish away the words
And their letters?
Let them fall off the letters
We made out of the leaves
And sent to each other
Under a sky a little less bleak.
Of course you've your reasons
Penned down in a letter
Unsent and unreceived,
Citing some (major) adjustments
To your blueprint of a perfect life
To account for one minor alteration
To that of mine.
We'll spare us the utterance
Of the what-ifs
And the could-have-beens
Let's be wary of
The usual suspects
Of killing with kindness.
It was a mistake to believe

In the myth of a perennial spring.
But now that we're disbelievers again,
Let's just say that it's winter's will
And we'll dissolve with the mist.

10. November 29, 2015

So, what do I do
With these rusty remnants
Of a daytime daze,
Burnt on my palimpsest?
I might still be able to trace
Your breath
And the shadow
You left while leaving.
When people have lived on far
Too less,
Who is to say
That it won't suffice?

11. Half-Life

She asked nonchalantly:
What was the half-life of a memory?
One-hundred and fifty-two days or so
And one-thousand and fifty-two nights.
He answers in a daze,
As he leaves scratches on a page.
It is the only sound in the sea of silence.
An unsung ode to obscurity.
And dreams of
Dawns and dusks,
And the first drizzles.
The dust settles when
A regiment of raindrops attacks
The sensibilities of a land long left barren.
Who are we
But solitary travelers in the ships of memory
Going against the tide of time?
What is the breeze to us?
Is it the fragrance of hope anew?
Or the smell of the fresh funeral flowers?
Who is to say when all is forsaken?
One more whiff of the forgetful air,

And the lofty sandcastles of yesteryear
Shall crumble with a trickle of time.
And all that is left unsaid
Shall end up washed away on a forgotten shore,
In a wistful half-smile.

12. Trellis

The waxy wings dissolve
During the very first flight
In the crimson sky,
As gravity gets a second wind.
A dream dies of despair,
Indifferent,
To shooting stars and wishing wells.
There's something a little too similar in this
To the finality of the fate of a fallen vine,
Right after the trellis breaks.

13. Seafarers' Serenade

Wrapping our breath
around our brittle hearts
to spring
a new lease of life
into the dying
night.
Fumbling about
with the arts
of the lost and the forgotten
flames of fiction,
we weave our way
around the wind,
with our white flags
turned into makeshift sails,
twin pieces of driftwood
deciding
to set for the shore.
I'll close my eyes
with the tide
one more time,
surrendering to your serenade
and shamelessly

ask for seconds.
As the night comes to a close,
I'll keep you company
in an awkward waltz,
with no one else around
to keep time.
And when our tongues are
too preoccupied to churn out
words,
I promise,
your touch shall have
the last word.

14. The Pieces Within

You made
an awkward autumn tumble
turn into a trapeze.
You blitzed on the tightrope
without the balance sheets
weighed by whats and hows and ifs
and moving still.
I forgot,
where we were,
where we'd left off,
in the debris
of love
and
other inconsequential things.
Is it really an ode to you
then,
or just our obituary?
I feel like an ocean,
where a thousand ships sank.
I find my arteries red with their rust,
and my tongue tied
to the taste

of a long-standing ardour,
that yet remains,
vainly obscured
beneath
dalliances evanescent.
A spectator on the sidelines,
a slave to his shadow,
shatters all that surrounds him
in the hall of mirrors.

15. The Intangible Mysteries of Loverspeak

Would it have been worth
the wait,
to read the textbook on love,
before you decided
to ditch caution,
and take your chances
before it might be too late?
For, between the lines
of love and hate,
no one ever told you
how bad it hurts
when you build your home
in a heart that's not your own,
and then after living there for a while,
you've to leave.
Far stranger than love
is loverspeak,
for when he said his heart
was yours forever,
he probably meant it

as a promise,
he thought he'd keep.
Truths turn into lies
post their expiration date.
It is,
more often than not,
transitory.
You probably wouldn't agree
that it all happened unintentionally.
You are lucky in a sense.
Wisdom after all,
is the sign of the weary.
Sitting through the remnants
of your spring,
ripe with regrets,
you'll look around the garden
blooming with breathing graves
and
you will want to die.
There's no pretty way
to put it any kind of poetry.
Fuck wordsmithery.
Just don't die,
but live,
instead.
For somewhat soon,
for the ones who hope,

the seasons pass by,
after playing some sad tunes
on repeat,
for a few thousand times
as your thoughts sleepwalk
for nights,
even the cacti bloom
when it's time,
and now it's time
for you to sleep,
my love.
Close your eyes,
and I will tell you my take
on the tale
of Rip Van Winkle,
and kiss you goodnight,
at the second sign of slumber,
before saying goodbye.
I will wait
for you to wake up
on some autumnal day,
after shedding your leaves
in your sleep,
with your branches bereft
of the yellow pages
of mirages of bygone hopes
and we will waltz

in the graveyard
to the sexton's song.
As your hair falls on your face,
momentarily unbound
from the darkness's allure,
take me to an empty grave
and put me to sleep
beneath the blaze
of the barren breeze,
that
breaks the spell
of the silence accrued
by your bleeding heart
over the long season
of gloom.

16. The Girl who Hated Getting Wet

She was the girl
who hated the rain
when it meant getting wet.
So I guess it irked me
to see her eyes
drenched
with a strange strain of regret
as she looked at me
for what I half-hoped to be
the last time.
We're all game
All in for the spark
but sometimes
the flames burn too bright
and duly the defenses turn up.
The coldness comes
through the part of your heart
you will never know you have,
taking self-preservation
to extreme means.

So it's not your fault,
probably,
to draw the curtains
and shun the sunlight out
when it got too warm,
I didn't expect you
to bake or burn a cake
on the flames.
But, you left instead,
changed your address.
This is all I said,
till I realized I'd digressed,
when all I think I wanted to say was
'It's not you, it's not me'.
The easiest thing
will be to blame it on biology.
So be it, but-
I wonder why the heart
gets the lion's share of the part
of the credit and the curses,
when it comes
to falling in and out of love.
Perhaps, my lungs are still in love
with the way you used to breathe
life into me,
with a bitter aftertaste
of coffee and cigarettes,

at night
after the nine to five.
I know it's not healthy.
Or maybe it's about the way
your toes curled,
as they touched mine,
when I absentmindedly caressed
the undercurrent of the silent scars
underneath your skin,
when your hands were yet mine
to hold.
You never rolled around much
in your sleep,
when you were with me.
Or maybe it's about...
Well, there are
a lot of maybes,
but none of them
are on the menu tonight,
save for an unforgettably
forgettable handshake,
and a smile,
and I guess that's all
we have to make do with
tonight.

17. Undramatic Monologue

I brushed off
the leftovers
of dust and despair
at the doormat,
on your doorstep.
Perhaps
all truths are terribly transient
but
the hesitating heart flutters
with a hope,
that
all worries about the world
shall
cease to exist,
on the cusp of your lips.
Why would I listen
to obsolete wisdom,
and learn to lose
this lofty expectation,
when the serenity

of your strength,
shined shyly,
betraying a gleam
of the wildness,
as you smiled.
Perhaps,
the weight of those words
of mine,
might not be that hard to bear
in time.
I'd plucked all the petals
of the poems previously written,
browsing through
the index of my insides,
to find appropriate references,
to corroborate the comfortable theory
of the circularity of life.
I found nothing,
but a bit of pity at the plight
of the poor poet,
and the needless need,
to hunt for metaphors
at night,
to tell you what I really feel.
So, I rummaged within
the reserves
of the weary would-be adventurer

and found a flurry of origami hearts
and paper planes.
Pick your favorite props
and let's do some flying
over the night sky,
hunting for meadows
and not metaphors
for a change,
pretending to parody
stareyed lovers
and write a script of our own,
on a palimpsest.
In that moment of make-belief,
there could be something more real
than the rest,
just as the solipssism
we shared
when our eyes met for once,
after firing fleeting stares
from cover.
Draw the curtains of your embrace,
as I shrug off the shyness
and lean in,
to hear your hair rustle,
as you come closer still,
to whisper a few words
in my ear.

Dramatic monologues are so done

anyway.

18. Of Soirees, Stalemates and Shopping for Bargains

I ran into you,
the other night,
on the edge of a street,
where I was wandering by.
You had traded your solitary strut
for slipping by the sides of strangers
of some kind of familiarity,
after another lap of loneliness.
It's dark,
but that almost qualified
as a quizzical glance.
I won't tell you the tale,
of the tamarind's taste,
and sour grapes,
or the origin story of
a make-belief man
making out with the memory
of lost love,
to a melancholy tune,
at night.

But last month,
I almost stopped by your stall,
to shop for some paper-weights,
searching for someone something
to stave off the wind,
its whispers and wails,
so that I am not undone,
as I wait for the tide,
to sail again.
In the flea market,
I found old coupons,
of favors from fickle friends
with benefits,
inside a teapot
that probably used to be yours,
with a faux antiquated finish,
and the scent or the stench
of countless cups of tea,
made in the madness
of the next morning's mist
that makes skeletal shadows
of someones or somemanys
brought to the bed
to make you feel like somebody again,
and not just someone else.
I too had built a home with my heart,
in my mind,

to play the part of the proverbial
finish line.
But, it slips. It doesn't suffice,
anymore,
to lay among bricks and stones
that languish in the loss
of the unsaid, the unmentioned
and the unmentionable things.
And the paint on the walls
is marred by whatever
that comes out when
souls bleed.
Strange,
the mysteries of metaphysical miseries.
So, I adjust
the rearview mirror of the convertible
in my imagination,
one last time as I leave,
not for someplace better,
but someplace else.
The door's closed,
not locked,
and I've left the light on,
to shine for somebody else,
perhaps,
in their hour of need,
who might stumble by,

wandering about,
someday,
searching for a place to call their home
or to just call it a day.

19. Tonight

I slipped right from the cusp of your lips,
like a ship missing the tide
But much worse,
Imagine it missing the last tide
for all time,
and you'd get closer
to where I am
emotionally. (slight laughter)
A serious stack of jenga,
A quintessential pack of dominos
and other stack related similes.
Anything at all that's about
the fall from atop.
I think I should question my need-
This silly desperate need
to play hide and seek
with these metaphors of mine
to tell you what I really feel.
It's not about telling you
that you're all I need
in this life of mine,
Or any other oft-mentioned words

from any lover's speech
from ancient times.
It's not about how washing
any cloth of questionable quality
makes its colors bleed
It's not about spite.
It's just about tonight.
What did I do but nothing,
Save for sleepwalking in the sun
and deck you with garlands of my words.
I'd have loved to play you like a saxophone,
with my fingers feeling their way to the highest notes,
Maddening up a mellow night
drenched in your favorite wine.
The wind wounds the wistful man
In a text of freedom.

20. Conscription Papers

The wicked war came
at our doorstep, via mail,
that washed up October morning.
An innocent bundle of papers,
with words in a magic weave,
put a spell on you,
and took you away from me,
and yourself.
You dissolved in a cloud of dust,
left by the transport truck,
when they came up with a cause.
And another evening
spent in an anxious wait
for something to change,
recedes,
as clusters of clouds
gather over cosmopolitan circuses.
Newspapers sell by numbers,
and I am tired.
The winter wizard,
with his wizened visage,
and a hardcover book,

offered us,
another chance at life after death.
So, I'll look for you,
beyond the bundle
of hurriedly filed MIA reports.
If you were here,
if you'd only stay,
for a second,
your fragile heart would do a double take,
as I disappear aboard that dreadnought,
setting sail,
away from myself.

21. Untimely Rains

I saw you,
walking past a million souls,
every evening spent,
seeking a silhouette shored up in a glade,
somewhere within this wasteland.
We were all walking round in circles,
stopping sometimes
to breathe in, and feel,
almost by accident.
While you were entwined,
in a helical hallucination,
and kept walking,
waiting for the climb.
You were out to master yourself,
but became a slave to your habit,
and built a tower,
to gaze at the world below.
When we first and last met,
I was a flame, half-extinguished,
languishing in the loss,
of an imagined raison d'etre.
Your lips parted ways

to welcome me like untimely rain.
Did I quench your thirst?
But I was never water.
I knew I'd leave
the same way I came
and nothing would change.
In this world,
with its patented sense of dissatisfaction,
I was there,
within that moment,
just on the outskirts,
of your solipsism,
And for all those talks
of chasing hallmark endings,
this will have to suffice.

22. The Address

I wrote you a letter on
the 27th of March,
and they marched in Madrid
on the 28th.
Its salutation, Dear Juan,
said all that preceded it,
of the lovelorn years you spent
in an arduous wait,
while I stuttered around
to find myself,
and of the mandarins you plucked
for me, from the same old tree,
when I was hungry.
It said
of the lamppost under which
I read your first letters,
and the stars
which for once seemed more
than distant dots on a distant sky.
You fought Franco, and won
a nameless pit where
I fear you now lie.

The darker clouds grow darker still,
as they take over the sky.
Now that it's over,
They'll make a murderer
and a martyr
out of you,
and all I've got to do,
is figure out a place,
where to send this letter.
I'll never post this unsent letter,
and I'd never know whom you fought for,
though you said it was for me,
and my freedom.
I know it's bad of me
to say this,
but I'm not too fond of ideologies.
Forgive me,
that I'm not selfless enough,
to make a martyr out of you.
Some might say that I'm just human.
But I never want to be called that again,
till I figure out the reason,
for all the absurdities of being human.

23. Cosmic Paint and Clouds of Smoke

Paint my sky-
the dreariest shade of grey
with the smoke streaming
out of your nose.
The chimneys
of that fictional factory
of childhood cheer,
still stand tall,
in obscurity.
Wave your wand
and conjure the clouds,
with an unhurried flurry
of smooth strokes and float
like a solitary silver lining
in my overcast sky.
Here's to the hope,
that the might of your madness
makes the clouds precipitate.
For, I've fallen for the way your words
tap dance across the street

to the sound of the falling rain
outside the window
of my solitary space.
I want to drag myself out
from the forlorn fortress
I built for my fragility,
when I see you walk barefoot
on uncharted terrain,
with the scratches and the scars
that leave no visible marks.
Yet the eyes illuminate
in the dark,
and bloom
because of the whiff
of the faraway breeze.
I want to walk with you.
We're after all,
old souls and dinosaurs,
mammoths in a haze
of bygone times,
relics of a Golden Age
that never dawned,
plunged
in a world's which is not
our own.

24. Bereft

A loss embittered,
served as dessert after the evening tea
with that old mistress of mine,
the road, of my return to home
at night.
A simple affair,
another missing case,
A tired policeman lodged
in the left of my brain,
refuses to entertain
the possibility of disappearance
of something beloved,
something innane.
The flowers have faded
to an ashen grey
and the weeds have woven
an echoing lack
in the words that come out
of a messy fountain pen,
a silent stammer,
drenched in grammar,
a sentence without a flaw

save for its being there.
The altar in autumn
is a cremation ground
in guise,
The gods have disappeared
at the sight
of the sacrificial lamb with tainted blood,
And it's time
to cremate the corpses of these wilted words,
and deal with the dead
before calling it a night.
I'd use a cheap lighter
to cremate the corpse
but the flames just
dance around
the derivative drivel,

25. Lamp Lights

Only the lonely
need to light up
their lamps
at night.
For,
you only sleep soundly
in the arms of others,
no matter what anyone
says.
You rummaged
your memories
to find some
olive branches
and offered them
to a hungry heart.
But they dance around with the wind.
Chaos is a catchy tune,
like a wildfire
on a silent night
like this.
As floundering ships
seek solace

in the sea
and the shore,
and the in between.
Their SOSs, duly sent out,
as the hourglass
runs out of hope,
return to sender,
unread
and unreceived.
The sad heart
leaves the loaded lifeboat
to save some souls
and sinks in the sea.
The sharks devour
the Good Samaritan.
It was a filling meal.
Light a lamp
for the departed.
Leave the door open,
and call it a night,
hungover on a dreary hope
to be haunted
again.
Some verses are
meant
to remain
incomplete.

Author's Bio

An avid bookworm, Arpan Naithani's experience in academia owing to his Masters in English along with his passion for banter in storytelling enables him to write with an insightful proficiency for the current generation. At present, he is working on the first iteration of a fantasy dystopia. "The Tale of a Paper Flower" is his first poetry collection featuring his original poems from 2015–19.

Printed by Libri Plureos GmbH in Hamburg,
Germany